Lightning Strikes

PIONEER EDITION

By Lesley J. MacDonald

CONTENTS

Lightnin Strikes

By Lesley J. MacDonald

Storm clouds move in. The sky turns dark. Flash! A bolt of lightning jumps from the sky.

You might not see lightning very often. But it is always hitting somewhere on Earth. About 100 bolts strike our planet every second.

Lightning is dangerous. It can cause many problems. Lightning can start forest fires. It can burn down buildings.

Lightning can also hurt people. Each year, it kills about 70 people. It injures around 300 others.

Staying Safe

Over time, people have looked for different ways to stay safe from lightning. Benjamin Franklin came up with one way in the 1750s. He made a **lightning rod.** It was pretty simple. But it worked.

Franklin put a metal pole on top of a building. He ran a wire from the pole to the ground.

Lightning struck. It hit the pole. Then it traveled along the wire into the ground. The building was not harmed!

Shocking Ideas. *RIGHT: Benjamin Franklin did tests during storms to learn about lightning. BELOW: These models helped Franklin make the lightning rod.*

Lightning Rods Today

People still use lightning rods today. The rods work just like the ones Franklin made. They sit on the tops of buildings. They carry lightning to the ground. Lightning rods keep buildings and people safe.

City Lights. *Lightning zaps the Empire State Building in New York City. A lightning rod at the top keeps the building safe from harm.*

© CLARENCE HOLMES PHOTOGRAPHY/ALAMY

NEW YORKER

5

Laser Power

Today, some people are looking for new ways to stay safe. A scientist named Jean-Claude Diels has an idea. He thinks **lasers** could help.

A laser is a machine. It makes a powerful beam of light. What do lasers have to do with lightning? Well, they just might work like lightning rods.

Diels wants to shoot a laser beam at storm clouds. He thinks lightning bolts will travel along the beam. Then they will go safely into the ground.

In the Lab

This idea sounds good. But why would it work?

Lightning is a bolt of **electricity.** That is a form of energy. Each bolt sends electricity through the air.

Lasers also send energy through the air. Their energy may **attract,** or pull, lightning to them. So lightning would follow the beams safely to the ground.

At least, that's what Diels thinks. The laser works in a lab. But Diels is not sure if it will work in a real storm. He is still testing it.

New Ideas

Testing the laser will take time. Diels thinks it will be worth the wait. Why? A laser can be shot at storms up to two miles away. So one or two lasers could protect a whole town.

In the future, lasers might keep people safe. But scientists are always coming up with new ideas. One day, someone may find another way to stay safe from lightning. Who knows? Maybe that person will be you!

Wordwise

attract: to pull toward

electricity: form of energy that can be seen when lightning strikes

laser: machine that makes a powerful beam of light

lightning rod: metal rod and wire used to carry a lightning bolt to the ground

What Makes Thunder Rumble?

Flash! You see a bolt of lightning. Boom! You hear thunder. Why does thunder follow lighting?

Lightning is superhot. A bolt heats the air to more than 43,000°F. Air is made of tiny parts called molecules. Lightning makes these tiny parts of air move quickly apart.

After lightning strikes, the air cools. The tiny parts of air move closer together again. The air moves so fast that it makes a sound. We call that sound thunder.

What Makes Lightning?

Lightning is a bolt of electricity. This electricity builds up inside clouds. Clouds are made of dust and water droplets. Wind blows the dust and droplets around inside the cloud. This makes a positive charge at the top of the cloud. It also makes a negative charge at the bottom.

The ground below a thundercloud has a positive charge. Lightning flashes between areas with positive and negative charges.

1. The top of a cloud has a positive electrical charge.

2. The bottom of a cloud has a negative electrical charge.

3. The ground has a positive electrical charge.

4. When the positive and negative electrical charges get strong enough, lightning flashes between the cloud and the ground.

5. Lightning also flashes between the top and bottom of a cloud.

Kinds of Lightning

Lightning comes in many different forms. Here are a few kinds you might see in your neighborhood.

5

4

3

Forked lightning looks like tree branches.

Sheet lightning is a flash of lightning inside a cloud.

Heat lightning is so far away that you cannot hear the thunder it makes.

Lightning Safety

Scientists are looking for new ways to keep people safe from lightning. You can also take steps to protect yourself. Here are some ways to stay out of lightning's path.

Staying Safe Outside

- **Check the weather.** Find out what the weather will be like. Stay home if a storm is on its way.

- **Find shelter.** Porches are not safe during a storm. Move indoors. Go inside a building.

- **Crouch down.** If you cannot find shelter, crouch down. Bend your knees and tuck your chest to your legs.

- **Stay away from trees.** Standing under a tree is not safe during a lightning storm.

- **Avoid metal.** Lightning can travel along metal fences and poles. During a storm, stay away from metal objects.

Staying Safe Inside

- **Move away from windows.** Glass does not protect you from lightning. Stay away from windows during a thunderstorm.

- **Stay off the phone.** Lightning can travel through phone lines. Make calls after a storm, or use a cordless phone.

- **Do not touch cords.** Lightning can travel through electrical wiring. Do not touch plugs or cords during a storm.

- **Wait to wash.** Lightning can travel along water pipes. Do not wash your hands or take a shower during a storm.

- **Wait until the storm ends.** Lightning can strike when you least expect it. Stay inside for 30 minutes after the last lightning.

Lightning

Answer these shocking questions to find out what you learned.

1 What makes lightning?

2 Why is lightning dangerous?

3 How does a lightning rod work?

4 How might a laser protect people?

5 How can you stay safe during a thunderstorm?